Internet DOs & DON'Ts

Keep Your Passwords Secret

Shannon Miller

PowerKiDS press™

New York

Published in 2014 by The Rosen Publishing Group, Inc.
29 East 21st Street, New York, NY 10010

First Edition

Editor: Jennifer Way
Book Design: Andrew Povolny

Photo Credits: Cover Adrian Pope/Photographer's Choice/Getty Images; p. 5 Thomas Barwick/ Photographer's Choice RF/Getty Images; p. 7 AVAVA/Shutterstock.com; p. 9 Thomas Barwick/Iconica/Getty Images; p. 11 iStockphoto/Thinkstock; p. 13 Tara Moore/Taxi/Getty Images; p. 15 Hemera/Thinkstock; p. 17 Fuse/Getty Images; p. 19 Comstock Images/Thinkstock; p. 21 Purestock/Getty Images; p. 23 Grady Reese/E+/Getty Images.

Library of Congress Cataloging-in-Publication Data

Miller, Shannon.
  Keep your passwords secret / by Shannon Miller. — First Edition.
    pages cm. — (Internet dos & don'ts)
  Includes index.
  ISBN 978-1-4777-1537-6 (library binding) — ISBN 978-1-4777-1562-8 (pbk.) —
ISBN 978-1-4777-1563-5 (6-pack)
  1. Computers—Access control—Passwords—Juvenile literature. 2. Internet—Security measures—Juvenile literature. I. Title.
  QA76.9.A25M5823 2014
  005.8—dc23
                                2012051004

Manufactured in the United States of America

CPSIA Compliance Information: Batch #S13PK4: For Further Information contact Rosen Publishing, New York, New York at 1-800-237-9932

Contents

There are lots of things to do online. You must use the **Internet** safely. This book will show you how to be safe.

You need a **password** to use some **websites**. A password is a secret word. A password should be easy for you to remember. It should be hard for others to guess.

7

A teacher or parent can help you make passwords. Passwords should have both letters and numbers. That makes them hard to guess.

Do not share your passwords. Keep your passwords secret! It is not safe to share your passwords.

A friend might ask to share passwords. Do not share your passwords with friends. They may promise to keep them secret. They might not keep that promise.

Some people steal others' passwords. They can do this if a password is easy to guess. This could cause you trouble if it happens.

15

Strangers can log in with your password. They can pretend they are you. They can see **private** facts about you. They can use those facts to hurt you.

Tell someone right away if your password is stolen. Tell a parent or teacher. He will know what to do.

You will need to make a new password. A trusted adult can help you do this. Do not share your new password.

You can be safe and have fun online. Keep your passwords secret. That is a big Internet do.

WORDS TO KNOW

Internet (IN-ter-net) A network that connects computers around the world. The Internet provides facts and information.

password (PAS-wurd) A string of letters and numbers that lets you use some websites.

private (PRY-vit) Not meant for strangers to know.

strangers (STRAYN-jerz) People you do not know.

websites (WEB-syts) Places on the Internet.

INDEX

WEBSITES

Due to the changing nature of Internet links, PowerKids Press has developed an online list of websites related to the subject of this book. This site is updated regularly. Please use this link to access the list:
www.powerkidslinks.com/idd/pass/

24